Carol Thomas-Weaver: Music Teacher

Published by
Twenty-First Century Books
38 South Market Street
Frederick, Maryland 21701

Text Copyright © 1991
Jennifer Bryant

Photographs Copyright © 1991
Pamela Brown

Printed in the United States of America

10 9 8 7 6 5 4 3 2 1

Cover and book design by Terri Martin

*Dedicated to all of the working moms
who helped with this project*

Library of Congress Cataloging in Publication Data

Bryant, Jennifer
Carol Thomas-Weaver: Music Teacher

Summary: Portrays the everyday life of a music teacher who is also
a busy mother.
1. Thomas-Weaver, Carol—Juvenile literature. 2. Women music teachers—
United States—Biography—Juvenile literature.
[1. Thomas-Weaver, Carol. 2. Music teachers. 3. Working mothers.]
I. Brown, Pamela, 1950- ill. II. Title. III. Series: Working Moms.
ML3930.T56B8   1991   372.87'092—dc20   [B] [92]   90-27864   CIP   AC   MN
ISBN 0-941477-56-8

Carol Thomas-Weaver: Music Teacher

Jennifer Bryant

Photographs by Pamela Brown

Photographic Consultant: Bill Adkins

TWENTY-FIRST CENTURY BOOKS

FREDERICK, MARYLAND

"A good Friday morning to you, boys and girls," the cheerful voice rings out through the classrooms of East Ward Elementary School.

It's the "good morning" voice of Carol Thomas-Weaver. Carol is a music teacher at East Ward. She instructs children from kindergarten to sixth grade about the different types of music, singing and listening skills, and musical instruments.

Like the other teachers at East Ward, Carol also helps out wherever she is needed. She especially likes to read the morning announcements over the school's public address system. Every morning at 9 o'clock, Carol turns on the microphone in the main office and gives the teachers and students a "wake-up call" for the new school day.

And like everything else she does, Carol finds a creative and interesting way to do this job. Have you ever heard someone add sound effects to the lunch menu? (Can you imagine what Carol does when they're having hot dogs for lunch?) Finding her own way to read the morning announcements—or to do any other job—is a big part of who Carol is and what she believes. "Be creative with everything you do," she says. "Make your life your own."

The teachers and students at East Ward are not the only people Carol has to wake up in the morning. There's Reggie, Jr., and his brother Malcolm. Carol is needed at home, too.

Carol Thomas-Weaver is a working mom.

On this chilly October morning, Carol awakens with a start. Her radio station is playing a noisy rap tune. "But wait a minute," Carol thinks. "That can't be my station." She checks the radio dial, and, sure enough, someone has set the alarm to a popular rap station. "Hmmm," Carol says to herself, "which one of them, I wonder?"

Carol quickly switches the station to one that plays only jazz. The soft strains of John Coltrane replace the heavy rhythms of M.C. Hammer. "Now I can start my day," Carol sighs.

You might think that someone who teaches music every day wouldn't want to hear another note at home. But Carol wouldn't think of spending her time at home without music. "Music isn't just something to listen to," she explains. "It's a way to express ourselves. Music isn't just something that's out there, on the radio or the concert stage. It's inside you, too. I could no more live my life without music than I could live without my own thoughts and feelings."

Carol's husband, Reggie, Sr., shares her interest in music. Reggie, Sr., has been playing the piano for many years. In the evenings, he often joins Carol for a living-room concert. "I can't think of a more peaceful way to close a hectic day," Carol says.

But right now the day has to get started.

This morning, a busy Reggie, Jr., passes his mother on his way to the kitchen. He seems to be talking to himself. "Alphabet," he says. "Let's see: A, L, P—"

"And what are you up to, young man?" Carol interrupts.

"Spelling test today, Mom," Reggie, Jr., replies, barely taking time to stop. "Dad promised to test me again this morning." Reggie wanders off, talking to himself again. "Now where was I?" he asks. "H, A, B . . ." Reggie heads downstairs to the kitchen, where he reviews his new words.

Carol watches Reggie, Jr., and wonders if he's the morning rap music culprit. "That gives me an idea," she says to herself. "What about using rap music to learn new spelling words?" A new song called "The Alphabet Rap" begins to play in her head as she peeks into Malcolm's room to make sure that he's awake.

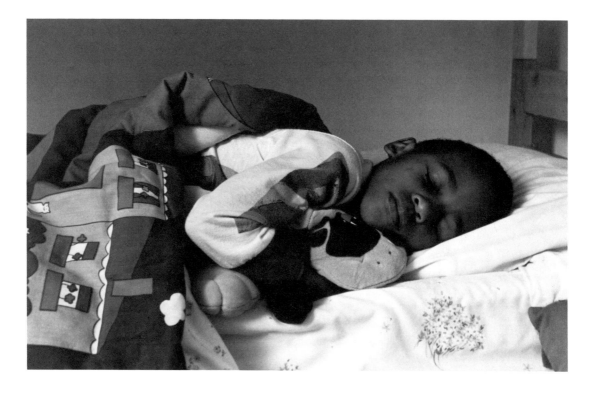

She's just about to ask her younger son, "Have you been fooling around with my morning music?" when she notices a pile of tissues next to Malcolm's nightstand.

"Are you getting a cold?" she asks with concern.

"I don't know," shrugs Malcolm. "My nose got stuffy last night." Carol puts her hands on Malcolm's face and thinks to herself, "No fever." But she takes his temperature just in case. "No fever," she announces this time.

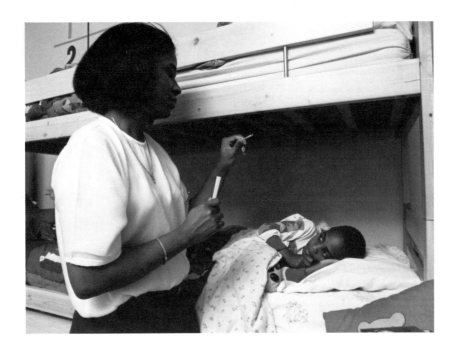

"I can go to school today," Malcolm quickly adds. He jumps out of bed and sniffles his way to the bathroom. Carol remembers staying home with Malcolm and Reggie, Jr., when they were sick. "It's always hard to return to work after missing several days. There's so much extra work to do," she thinks. "But that's part of being a working mom."

"The family comes first," Carol says. "That's the rule in this household."

Another rule in this household is that everyone helps out around the house. Taped to the kitchen door are "Job Charts" for Reggie, Jr., and Malcolm. There's a place on the charts for them to mark whenever a job is done. Malcolm's morning job is to get himself dressed for the day—or, at least, to try.

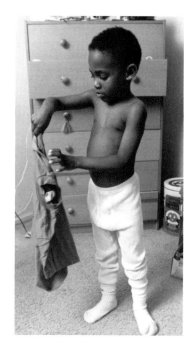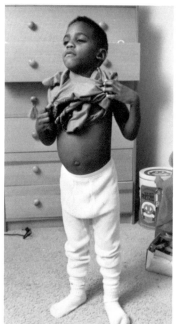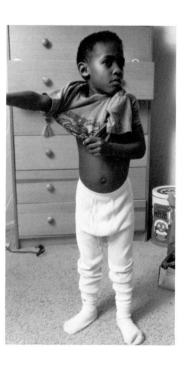

Because Reggie, Jr., is the oldest, one of his jobs each morning is to help Mom get breakfast on the table.

Today, it's oatmeal, toast, and juice for the boys. While the boys are eating breakfast, Reggie, Sr., helps his older son with his homework.

Carol barely has time for toast and jam before driving the boys to the Rocking Horse Day Care Center. Malcolm stays here for the day. His older brother stays only for the first hour. Then he rides the bus to school. Reggie, Sr., picks the boys up at the end of the day.

On the way to the day-care center, Carol listens to Reggie, Jr., practicing his spelling words. "A, U, S, T—" he says and pauses. "Mom," he asks, "where is Australia, anyway?" Carol also listens to Malcolm sniffling and wonders whether he should really go to school today.

Carol took a year off from teaching after Reggie, Jr., was born. And she took another year off after giving birth to Malcolm. When it was time to return to work, she had mixed feelings. "Even now," Carol admits, "it's hard to leave them for the day, though I know that they're having a good time. But I guess these feelings are part of being a working mom, too."

Another part of being a working mom is sharing housework and chores with her husband. Carol and Reggie, Sr., share the work at home. They call it "equal parenting." Reggie says: "We're a team. I make the lunches, and she makes dinner. I wash the clothes, and she folds and puts them away. Carol does the grocery shopping, and I put the food away. We know how important it is to divide up the chores. When both parents work outside the home, there has to be sharing inside the home."

Carol enjoys being a music teacher. It's her job to teach young people the basic elements of music: melody (the arrangement of musical sounds, or notes), tempo (the speed at which music is played), rhythm (the patterns of short and long sounds), and harmony (the way two or more sounds go together). She teaches her students about different instruments, ways of writing songs, and musical traditions.

But "Mrs. Weaver," as the students call Carol, sees her job as more than that. "Of course, I want my students to learn certain basic ideas and skills that will help them enjoy music—and maybe make music a permanent part of their lives. But I don't expect all of them to become musicians. There's really so much more to learn about music and so many different ways to enjoy it."

When Carol teaches about sounds, or rhythm, or tempo, she's really teaching children about new ways to express themselves. "Music is a creative outlet," she says. "It's a form of self-expression. Music is a way of understanding yourself and explaining yourself to others. And it's also a way of changing yourself and the way you think and feel. That makes music a very powerful force. Too many people today, including far too many young people, use dangerous things, like drugs, to change how they think and feel. The way I see it, music and the other arts are healthy choices for young people to make."

Mrs. Dana's kindergarten class troops into Carol's room at 9:05 A.M. Carol leads this eager group to the front of the room, where they sit on the floor beneath a picture of a huge house.

"Today," Carol begins, "we're going to learn about different sounds." Carol points to one of the rooms of the house. "Imagine someone your age just waking up this morning. What kinds of sounds do you think might come from this room?"

Yawns and stretches come from these five-year-olds, who not too long ago were yawning and stretching in their own bedrooms.

"Very good," Carol says, as she points to the top of the stairs that lead to the first floor of the imaginary house. "Now our friend is walking down the stairs to the kitchen." A picture of Reggie, Jr., on his way to breakfast as he spells out "alphabet" crosses Carol's mind—and a smile crosses her face. But the same picture makes her think about Malcolm, and Carol worries about his cold. "You don't stop being a mom when you're on the job," Carol says.

Carol turns her attention to the class. "What kinds of sounds do you think these old stairs would make?"

Every kind of creak and squeak and groan can be heard creaking and squeaking and groaning from Mrs. Dana's class. And there's another sound that's often heard in Carol's music classes. It's the sound of laughter. It's the sound of children having fun.

"I want my students to have a good time," Carol says. "But I want them to learn, too. And for that to happen, I have to keep an orderly classroom." Carol makes sure each student reads the "Rules and Consequences" chart and knows what behavior is not permitted. Her rules are simple and fair:

CLASSROOM RULES

1. Follow directions 1st time given!
2. Raise hand before speaking.
3. Walk, don't run in the classroom.
4. Never mistreat an instrument!
5. Do not play your instrument until you are told!!!

CONSEQUENCES

1st time student breaks a rule: Name on board
2nd time: ✓check beside your name - 15min recess
3rd time: recess detention. (full)
4th time: Danger Zone . . .

"Classroom rules help teachers set limits," says Carol. "And they teach children that it's important to respect each other's right to learn. Of course, it's important for children to know that learning can be fun, too."

As Carol moves her finger from room to room, her young students *do* have fun making every kind of sound imaginable. And they're learning an important lesson, too, though they may not know it yet. When Carol is done with the pretend house, she turns to a nearby collection of instruments. One by one, she shows how these instruments can make sounds like the ones her students just made. A violin can sound like that creaky staircase! And doesn't that bassoon sound just like a "good morning" yawn?

"The music we make with instruments," Carol says, "is part of the music all around us. It's part of the music we make with our lives." Carol uses many different activities to teach young people about the world of musical sounds.

Another sound suddenly makes itself heard loud and
clear. It's the sound of the school bell announcing that music
class is over for this kindergarten group. Carol wishes
everyone a happy and music-filled day.

In the bright faces of her students, Carol can see herself when she was a little girl. Carol grew up with her mother and younger sister, Kathy. Her father died when she was only ten years old. So Carol had a lot of helping out to do.

"My mother was counting on me," recalls Carol, "and I wanted to do whatever I could to make life easier for her. I didn't mind looking after my younger sister. In fact, I was proud that Mom trusted me to take care of Kathy."

Both Carol and Kathy went to public schools near their Philadelphia neighborhood. It was in junior high that Carol first thought about becoming a teacher. "I always looked up to my teachers," she remembers. "I admired how much they knew and how easily they could present that knowledge to others. In my eyes, a teacher was someone to respect."

"At first, I wanted to be an English teacher," Carol continues. "But, in seventh grade, I began learning how to play the flute. I spent more and more time practicing, and I joined the school band. Gradually, music became my main interest. From then on, I wanted to become a music teacher."

At the end of junior high, Carol had a big decision to make. Most of her friends were going to the neighborhood high school. But some of Carol's teachers thought that she should go many blocks away to Overbrook High, a school with special programs in music, painting, dance, and drama. Carol wanted to stay with her friends, but she wanted to continue her music training, too. It was a tough choice.

To be accepted to this new "high school of the arts," Carol would have to pass an audition. An audition, or tryout, is an individual performance by an artist to show his or her ability. Carol decided to audition and see what happened. When she received the news that she had passed the audition and was accepted to Overbrook High, she felt a sense of pride and accomplishment. Her decision was made! It would mean leaving close friends and a familiar world behind, but Carol knew that she wanted to study music.

Fortunately for Carol, one close friend wasn't left behind for long. The year after Carol started attending Overbrook, her sister was accepted for music training, too. Now they could share the long trip to school. Each morning, Carol and Kathy would pack their books, lunches, and musical instruments for the six-block walk to the nearest bus stop. From there, they rode the bus to the center of the city, where they boarded a trolley (an electric streetcar) for the rest of the way to school. The whole trip often lasted an hour.

But at least they had each other for company. "We weren't just sisters," Carol says. "We were best friends. The fact that Mom was working so hard each day to provide for us brought us closer together. We knew it wasn't easy for her, and we were determined to do our best, at home and at school. This was our way of helping out. And our common interest in music helped us form a close bond."

"We supported and encouraged each other," she says.

After her first morning class, Carol has a "free" period for preparing lessons. For each grade level, Carol has a different set of goals. Mrs. Dana's five-year-olds are learning about different sounds. The second-grade and third-grade students are learning about the different ways sounds can be put together. And the older students in Mr. Jenkins' sixth-grade class are learning about the different groups, or families, of instruments that make up an orchestra: the strings, the woodwinds, the brass family, and the percussion instruments. A "free" period gives Carol a quiet time to think about her goals and design lessons for each class.

But it's never quiet for very long. Today, Carol is interrupted by several members of the school chorus. Carol is directing the choral program for the winter assembly, and several students would like some help with their parts.

Carol works closely with each student—advising one to hold a note a few more seconds, showing another how to develop a more open and richer sound ("Bigger breaths," Carol says), and reviewing the lyrics, or words, to the songs with a third student.

As Carol listens carefully to her students sing, she is reminded of her own music training. Carol earned a degree in Music Education at Temple University in Philadelphia. To earn her degree, she had to take a variety of courses both in music performance (with an emphasis on the flute) and in methods of teaching music.

After graduating from college, Carol would often perform at parties or special events with her sister Kathy. They even wrote and recorded their own music. In fact, one of their musical pieces, a song called "This Moment," was played at Carol's wedding.

More than 20 years later, both Carol and Kathy are still involved with music. Kathy is a professional violinist and songwriter. Carol's musical career took her in another direction. "I always knew I wanted to teach," she says. "I love children and working with young people too much to have considered doing anything else."

"That's why I became a music teacher instead of a professional musician," Carol says. "But I'm proud of my sister and her work—and I know she's proud of me."

Taking pride in your work is important to Carol. She takes pride in her teaching and in the efforts of her music students. "Watching a nervous student sing alone for the first time," Carol says, "or watching a class discover the beauty of harmony—those times make a difference."

For Carol, "music is a way to express ourselves—our own thoughts and feelings. Musicians use sound the way painters use color: to make a statement about how the artist is thinking or feeling. I try to help my students understand this. I ask them to think about why they like the types of music they do. 'How does the music make you feel? What do you think the person who wrote it was feeling?' When my students can answer such questions, they see that music is more than sound. It's something that's inside of them!"

Taking pride in your family is important to Carol, too. She takes pride in watching her young boys find their own forms of self-expression. "I encourage Reggie and Malcolm to make their own choices. I don't want them to think they have to be involved in music just because I am." Carol remembers the rap beat that woke her up this morning. "Of course, I prefer some forms of self-expression to others."

Carol works closely with the members of the choral group until she hears the sound of footsteps coming toward her room—third-grade footsteps to be precise. It's Mrs. Bates' class. They've been working on tempo and harmony, and Carol starts the class quickly on a rousing note. "Let's warm up with the song we've been practicing," she suggests. Carol steps to the piano and raises her hands for the first note. At once, 25 voices begin to sing "Little 'Liza Jane," a traditional African-American folk song:

Come, my love,
And go with me,
Little 'Liza Jane.

As the students sing, they use body movements—clapping their hands, snapping their fingers, slapping their thighs—to emphasize the rhythm of the song.

"That was pretty good," Carol says. "Now let's try it with some of the new tempos we learned in our last class." Carol begins to play the piano at a different speed. "Allegro!" she shouts.

"What?" one student whispers.

"Faster!" a friend whispers back. "Faster!"

Again, 25 voices begin to sing, but this time it seems that the song is sung at 25 different speeds. It's clear that the class needs more practice at changing the tempo of a song. There are many different musical tempos from a very slow speed (like "largo") to a very fast one (like "prestissimo"), and Carol gets her students used to changing speeds with special games and teaching techniques.

One of her favorite techniques is to have a group of students stand in a circle and pass a beanbag around in time to the music. As the tempo of the music changes, the students have to pass the beanbag more slowly or more quickly.

"It's a kind of game," Carol says, "and a fun way to learn."

Carol has a surprise for this group today. "It's time for us to become composers," she says. "A composer is someone who writes a song. We're going to compose a Halloween song." Carol plays some basic melodies, and the class decides on one that has a slow, almost creepy beat.

Next, they choose sound effects to add a sense of mystery and horror. There are many different suggestions: people screaming, werewolves howling, dogs barking, ghosts moaning, and witches cackling. One student shows the class how to make the sound of footsteps coming closer . . . closer . . . closer.

Everyone has ideas for the words, or lyrics, to the song. And Carol insists that everyone's ideas be treated with respect. One student lists the suggestions on the blackboard.

At last, the song is written. Now it's time for the actual performance. The class rehearses the melody and lyrics; then they add the sound effects. After several tries, Carol thinks they're ready to record. She pushes the "start" button on the tape recorder. The song goes like this:

Halloween is coming soon:
(sound of ghosts moaning)

Witches ride on their brooms,
(sound of witches laughing)

Ghosts and goblins everywhere,
(sound of footsteps coming closer)

Giving you a deadly scare!
(sound of people screaming)

Carol rewinds the tape and plays it for the class. "That sounds really good!" she says.

"Do you think it's good enough to play on the morning announcements?" one student asks.

"We shall see, my little friends," Carol replies with a scary, witchy cackle. "We shall see."

31

The bell announces that the class is over. Carol teaches four more classes before the day (and another long week) is over, too.

For Carol, each day is a
special day, a chance to
share her own love of music.

But by the time the last bell
of the day rings, Carol is ready
for a weekend away from drums
and tambourines and beanbags
and imaginary houses making
imaginary noises.

But the day is not quite over for Carol. After school, she drives to St. Paul's Baptist Church, where she directs choir practice. "Music is an important part of the religious service at St. Paul's," Carol explains. "It's a language of worship that everyone can understand and share. Music helps to bring everyone at St. Paul's together."

"Imagine a world without music," Carol says.
"Whether or not we are aware of it, our lives are enriched
by music. Music helps to reveal the nature of human
feelings. It is truly a universal and unifying factor in
our lives."

By the time Carol gets home, it's dark outside. But the lights at home are turned up bright, the stereo's turned up good and loud, and Carol knows just what's going on. It's another raucous Friday night. At the Thomas-Weaver house, Friday night is a time for letting loose, making some noise, and having fun.

Reggie, Jr., and Malcolm lead the band as they lip-synch their favorite songs. They're hot tonight!

Carol and Reggie, Sr., show the boys a few steps of their own.

When Mom and Dad collapse on the sofa, Malcolm turns the stereo to his favorite station. Suddenly, a deep rap beat starts to rock the house.

"Aha!" Carol exclaims. "So you're the good morning rap music culprit. I should have known."

But even Friday night has to come to an end. Carol and Reggie, Sr., get the boys ready for bed. Once they have been tucked in and given a good-night kiss, Mom and Dad sneak downstairs for a few moments together.

Reggie, Sr., plays a quiet tune on the piano. Carol joins him on the flute. The house is filled with the soft sound, and a deep and lovely peace.

"I can't think of a better way to end the day," Carol says.

Glossary

allegro	a fast musical tempo
audition	a tryout by a performer to show his or her ability
brass instruments	a group of wind instruments made of brass, such as the trumpet and trombone
composer	a person who writes songs
harmony	the way two or more musical sounds go together
instrument	a device for producing musical sounds
largo	a very slow musical tempo
lyrics	the words to a song
melody	an arrangement of musical sounds, or notes
note	a musical sound
orchestra	a group of musicians who play together on string, woodwind, brass, and percussion instruments
rhythm	a pattern of short and long sounds in music
percussion instruments	a group of instruments played by being struck or shaken, such as the drum and xylophone
prestissimo	a very fast musical tempo
strings	a group of stringed instruments, such as the violin and cello
tempo	the speed at which music is played
woodwinds	a group of wind instruments, such as the oboe and flute

DUE DATE

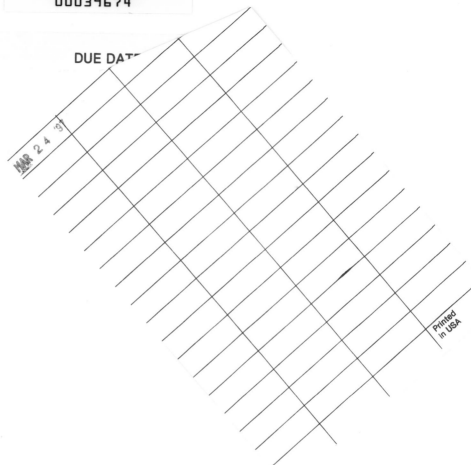

MAR 24 '97

Printed
in USA